A RAY
OF HOPE

The Story of Timothy Young's
Inspiring Journey
Through Captivity and his Deliverance by God.

TIMOTHY YOUNG

authorHOUSE®

AuthorHouse™
1663 Liberty Drive
Bloomington, IN 47403
www.authorhouse.com
Phone: 1 (800) 839-8640

Published by AuthorHouse 08/20/2019

ISBN: 978-1-7283-2419-7 (sc)
ISBN: 978-1-7283-2418-0 (e)

Print information available on the last page.

This book is printed on acid-free paper.

Contents

Prologue

HOPE - it begins with the striking of a match in the darkest void. The spark becomes a glimmer of flickering light transforming into a tiny flame with a hot blue heart. Shadows recoil, fleeing from the growing beacon as the light expands consuming the darkness until only the glow of holy fire remains.

This is the birth of hope. Hope is the bearer of healing light. Reaching into the darkest recesses of your mind, hope's flame guiding you out of the abyssal realm of fear and despair. Hope gives birth to faith, restoring your mind and body. Regardless of pain or suffering, hope releases you from illness, physical debilitation and depression. Above all, restoring your soul and ever guiding you towards the ultimate light of hope.

My name is Timothy Young. This is the story of how God delivered me and made me a witness to the true power of hope. Since birth, like Job, my life story has been a testament of trial and tribulation. And, how my steadfast faith in God gave me the strength to endure the years of torment at the hands of Satan. Even though, I came near to death many times and Satan found many ways to torment me through illness, mental anguish, and supernatural intervention. Also, like Job, I remained faithful to God. Never losing sight of His true calling. The greatest calling, my life's mission, to be a light bringer and messenger of hope.

CHAPTER 1

My Humble Beginnings and The Start of My Inspired Journey

To truly understand my beginnings you must first get to know my mother. It was through her unshifting faith and love for Christ. As well as, her example of Him here on earth that shaped me and my faith into what it is today. It is only through the value she gave to my life that I am here and able to bring that same value to the lives of others.

My mother, Ella Mae Rand, was born on May 10, 1938, in Stafford, Alabama. She was one of eight children. Her father abandoned her when she was eight and she lost her mother at the age of ten. My mother had little memory of her father. It was not uncommon, at the time, for many black men to abandon their families to find what they thought were better lives up north. This left many women and children to struggle, unsupported, alone for day to day survival.

Back then it was typical for orphaned siblings to be separated and sent to different homes. Unfortunately, the family that took her were extremely strict and heartless. Her upbringing was cold and abusive. She was frequently punished both at home and school, which she only attended until ninth grade. It was a great time of hardship for my mother. She survived on little food and faced an endless routine of housework and caring for the family's other children. As was common also in those days, my mother worked as a maid for white clients also picking cotton. She eventually found work in a local cafe.

With no family nearby and no love from her foster family, she suffered from isolation and loneliness. She missed her mother and memories of her happier childhood. Often overwhelmed by mistreatment she would take refuge behind a barn to cry out to her. Memories of her mother were deeply rooted in her helping shape her faith and great love for Jesus. She carried His spirit with her and believed in always doing right by others.

What can I say about my mother? In spite of all of the hardship she endured, she did not allow it to turn her into a bitter hardened individual; like those who had mistreated her. She, being a true woman of faith, allowed these lessons to shape her into a true angel in human form. The embodiment of Christ's love here on earth. She was the sweetest, most compassionate woman with an infectious smile that instantly warmed your heart. Her smile gave you peace, reassurance, and comfort like you've never known. She had so much love in her heart. It shone like a torch in the darkest night to guide you to a safe place. A light bringer and generous giver of hope. And she was generous enough through her love and faith to pass this gift onto me.

Despite the growing racial tension in the South during the tumultuous times of the civil rights movement, especially in Selma, her greatest gift was a love that broke down barriers. Perhaps it was her goodness and devotion to God that people sensed in her. When she passed away, it seemed like the entire world attended her funeral. Even those who normally never associated with black people came. Many of those who had been contributors to the racial tension, inequality, and instability; through racism, segregation, and disrespect. Which is a testament to how strong my mother's influence was because of her great love for Christ.

My mother met my father at the cafe where she worked. His name was Cleveland Ohio. He was also born in Stafford and worked for the railroad. At the time my mother had five children by another man. My father was separated and had children from that relationship. While my parents were together, they had me and my two brothers.

My father was never truly involved in our lives because he already had a family. He wasn't much of a parent or provider, preferring to keep to himself, he also tended to drink occasionally. This in no way made him a bad person. He just wasn't there for us. My parents soon grew apart because of his other relationship, as well as, his tendency to philander.

After hurting his back not the job, my father retired in 1981 and permanently moved back to his farm in 1983.

My mother told us not to be bitter towards him, even though, he did not give us as much fatherly support as he should have.

By 1988 I had a car so I visited my father. Spending time talking to and praying for my father through his declining health, until his death in 1993.

My mother's faith remained strong despite my father's abandonment, a traumatic childhood, poverty, racism, bearing a stillborn child, and raising eight children alone. She was an inspirational influence on us and everyone around her. If anyone epitomized the power of hope, it was surely her.

Her love for us was unconditional. She always motivated us to do well in school so we could better ourselves and pursue our goals. Working three jobs, she did her best to provide a life for us free from the struggle she endured as best she could. Firm and loving, often sacrificing sleep and nourishment for herself to ensure all of our needs were met.

It was unbelievably difficult for me to stay with my mother during her last days because I couldn't bear to deal with her impending death. I was so depressed, broken, and defeated. I felt on the brink of death myself.

A few days before my mother's death I experienced a vision from God. It was more of a tribute of her life, showing me her life journey and all the sacrifices she made for us. Though she drew near to death, she looked like a floating angel. Her skin bore the most divine golden radiance, glowing like the face of Moses on his return from Mount Sinai. She was illuminated by the supernatural love of God. His glory was on her and she knew it. I then saw her smiling as she ascended into heaven. It was beautiful, yet, terrifying and heart wrenching. Though to most ordinary people visions like these would seem comforting. For me, every breath of every moment was torture bringing me ever closer to what would be the darkest day of my life.

I remember my mother's last words to me the night before she died. "When you can't call on me, call on Jesus." Even now I hear her saying her favorite phrases…"Give me flowers while I'm living." And "A bushel, a peck, and a hug around the neck."

The next day, she was called to be with the Lord, reading

her Bible in her favorite chair. I still see the image of her in my mind and kept the shroud she was wrapped in.

Already suffering from the worst chronic depression of my life when my mother died. The added torment of losing her plunged me into an abyss of brokenness and devastation like never before. It was as if I had experienced my own death and now resided in an eternal hell of constant depression and anxiety. A vicious cycle of weeping, starvation, and sleep deprivation left me in an anguish that swallowed up all light within me like quicksand. During these lowest moments, the demonic forces already preying on my mind whispered seductively of suicide and how easy it would be to just end my own suffering.

My mother's funeral was on Saturday. I, by the grace of God, found the strength to make the funeral arrangements and deal with her burial. The epic attendance was only a testament to how many people loved her and all the lives she had blessed with hers. The endless stream of loving faces, words, condolences, hand shakes, shared tears, embraces did nothing to comfort me. I desired to join her in the coffin. Just the thought of never seeing her again, of hearing her voice or seeing her sweet face extinguished the flame in my heart.

The next day I reached my ultimate breaking point. I was an emotional nervous wreck at the end of my rope. That Sunday I prayed to God begging Him to help me because I could no longer bear the torment of my life. Death became more attractive. I wanted to just give up and let the darkness take me that was beckoning me into it. I told Him if He didn't help relieve my burden...then, I heard a whisper. At that moment, the phone rang. God had answered my prayers. It was a woman from Tuscaloosa inviting me to Holiness Church. Deep in my soul I knew this was not a coincidence. The phone call saved my life and also completely altered it.

I barely had the strength to drive to the church. The female pastor noticed my distress and talked with me. I was so defeated I could hardly respond. She asked me if I died now what would I have accomplished with my life. She could see that I was a man of God, with great purpose, who had lost my way after my mother's death and thirty-five years of struggling with my gifts. She asked me if I'd like to be healed. I told her I wanted to get baptized and repent of my sins.

When she touched me and anointed me with oil, suddenly I felt the explosive power of God rush through my body. Brilliant light, so intense, it purged all sickness and demonic forces from me like a divine sledgehammer.

This truly was my Lazarus moment, when God healed and anointed me. He literally rescued me. Raised me from the dead. I was born again. God engulfed me with His light and resurrected me through His power. The new life force He bestowed upon me was like the power of the sun. The essence of life that banished all demonic spirits attached to me. In these supernatural moments, God cleansed every physical and mental ailment, torment, and pain that kept me in bondage for so many years.

I came out of it a brand new man. God's healing gave me a strong, clear mind, a new sense of determination and purpose. My rebirth healed and empowered me. God had truly entered me and I became a conduit for Him, sharing the healing He bestowed upon me on others.

While my mother's faith and prayers gave me the hope to survive until her death. God filled the void left by her passing and saved me. I had now experienced heaven on earth because God had touched me and given me hope. Helping me to realize my path and potential. And, that is to share the message of His power and glory with the world.

Chapter 2

Illness, My Struggle with Realizing My Calling

I still recall the feeling of hot sand under my bare feet as I walked along the sandy road that humid Alabama day in August 1972. The sight of lush cotton fields, abundant orchards, and fertile pecan groves soothed me. Though it was still early, the day promised to be a scorcher. I felt a trickle of sweat begin to run down my spine beneath my worn, faded, T-shirt and overalls. It didn't matter. The peaceful serenade of song birds in the background as the warm sun lovingly kissed my face, reminded me I was alive. Gratitude overwhelmed me. I was feeling better and no longer needed to be confined to a bed.

The last three months had been a nightmarish battle with asthma. The unimaginable fear and pain of always feeling as if my lungs were constricted by iron bands was the reality I lived in for the first thirty-five years of my life. Until, God healed me.

For those of you who have ever wondered what it is like to experience the terror of asthma, imagine perpetually drowning. Feeling each breath is your last. Your heart labors to assist your scarred, ravaged, lungs to pump oxygen to the rest of your pain wracked body. You gasp and wheeze, gulping for precious air as you hover on the edge of consciousness. You are literally suffocating, as if someone placed a bag over your head. A torment beyond fathom. Leaving your body weak and fatigued, kissing the face of death with every painful inhale.

Everyday becomes an ordeal when something as simple as breathing is a constant challenge. It was worse at night. At least during the day light felt like a reassuring hand. But with the darkness of night came the tangible presence of fear taunting me with the ever illusive question…would I survive the night or not?

Medications could not cure my illness. I was allergic to seventy-two substances, most of which actually triggered my asthma. The ones I could take only relieved the constricting pressure on my lungs. Inhalers only helped temporarily, as well as the entire regime of medications I was on for my COPD; which was another by-product of my condition. As a result, I grew from a sickly infant into a sickly child.

As a person born with hereditary breathing difficulties, asthma was only the beginning of many tribulations to enter my life. It affected me more severely than anyone else in my family. We all, including my parents and siblings, suffered from health issues. These ranged from high blood pressure, diabetes, to milder forms of asthma. Though most of my brothers and sisters grew out of it, I was particularly more susceptible to illness due to my delicate immune system.

It was not only the physical suffering that plagued me in the early stages of my life. Due to the fact I spent so much of my early years on the nebulous borders between life and death, I often saw visions of spirits and otherworldly creatures. When I was seriously ill, angels came to me along with other visions I couldn't explain.

This gave me an ever increasing sense of how different I truly was from my peers and others around me. For fear of being accused of practicing voodoo or some other dark art, I couldn't discuss the discovery of my gifts with anyone outside of my family. Particularly, my aunt who shared my ability of discernment. I soon learned I had no choice but to experience these visitations.

Sensing I was different, most other children didn't interact with me. I was teased and shunned. Not even my junior high principal liked me because he sensed how unlike the other children I was. Perhaps it was the pack mentality that causes people to group together to attack or drive out what they are afraid of most, what they cannot understand. Sometimes I was unjustly accused of doing things although I was too weak to cause any trouble.

I truly began to realize my gift, when I realized I had the ability to look into the souls of others and see who they really were. Later on, I would become ill from taking on the illnesses of others during the healings. I often got marks under my eyes or my features changed completely because of their afflictions. I was still the same person but my altered appearance disturbed many people.

Because of my developing gifts, I was often too weak to play and attending school became an issue. Even though, I was a bright student who enjoyed and was eager to learn, my physical weakness became an obstacle that caused me to fall behind and my grades to suffer. My siblings were all in different grades, so they did not bare witness to what was going on. I had to suffer in silence. Believing if others would simply look past my outer appearance, they would discover the beauty of my inner spirit.

All I wanted was to be well and happy like the others. I desired acceptance, to have friends, and no longer be ostracized for my perceived frailty.

Many nights I cried myself to sleep after a difficult day. Asking God why He punished me like this. All the while, my mother when she heard me crying would gather me in her arms, rocking me to sleep as we prayed together. Before I had truly discovered the greatness of the gift He had bestowed upon me. And, He only gives his toughest battles to his strongest warriors. I reached an epiphany. Yet as Jesus suffered on the cross for the sins of man, my suffering was a revelation of the mission God had placed before me. It would be my duty and privilege to honor Him through this gift.

CHAPTER 3

Physical Debilitation is Often More Than Physical

In addition to the suffering caused by my chronic asthma, I endured yet another attack on my body. This manifested itself as the affliction of blindness at age seven and it would continue until I was fourteen. Triggered by years of allergies and environmental irritants, I developed lesions and cataracts on my irises that eventually became infected.

Coupled with my asthma and allergies that required shots, I was overwhelmed with pain and discomfort. My eyes had sunken to the point where they looked inhuman. I was forced to wear eye patches and be led around because of my blindness. This discomfort was only secondary to the almost supernatural burning that felt like hot pokers in my eyes. To say it was agony, barely conveys what I endured.

During this time of my life, it seemed I was always going to the doctor. My world had shrunk to the sterile confines of waiting and exam rooms. Although my family didn't have a car, and my mother worked three jobs and could not always take me herself; she was determined to make sure I received treatment. Yet, no matter how many doctors I saw, none could provide an accurate diagnosis regarding the cause of this terrible affliction on my eyes. Of course, I knew it was more than just a new physical ailment. It was a demonic attack.

While my health presented constant challenges since birth, the thought of losing my sight altogether filled me with great fear. I was already severely limited by asthma and my weak physical condition. To face further restrictions on my mobility, to not be able to run and play, or even something as simple as look at the sky or the faces of my family was the ultimate test of my faith in God.

As always, the nights were the worst. So many times I lay in bed, struggling for breath, my view of the world hobbled by darkness. Both my lungs and eyes burned. Finding any peace or comfort was impossible. This is when the demons came to taunt me. This is when they fed on my vulnerability. Like rats, they endlessly sought a crack to slide through and claim my soul.

Even though my blindness prevented me from physically seeing these minions of Satan, I felt the coldness of their presence, heard their infernal whispering. That my brothers slept nearby was no deterrent. They weren't discerners, and were spared the torment of existing on the border of light and darkness. In my bed, I was as isolated from them as a castaway on a remote island.

When I reached my lowest point of despair, angels appeared to me, and I was saved by the prayers of my mother and the community as they saw my calling. As a discerner, if God chose me to deliver a message to the world, if He used me to convey that his love manifest in miracles through the power of belief, it was my duty to fulfill that mission.

"Help me, Father," I whispered in the darkness. "Help

me be the servant you chose me to be. Give me the strength fight the demons and speak Your words."

My mother prayed constantly for my healing alone and with other community members. She sensed when the demons were attacking me and often took me into her room to pray with me. We knelt by her bed and bowed our heads. Holding hands, we prayed together.

"Help him, Jesus," she prayed. "Heal him so that he may bring your light to the world. Protect him from the evil that covets his power. Help him, Jesus. Amen."

Since the doctors at the Selma clinic couldn't help me, they referred me to the Children's Hospital at the University of Alabama Birmingham for treatment. A round trip of over three hours, the journey was long and exhausting. When my blindness was at its worst, my last resort for treatment was the Eye Foundation in Birmingham.

Simply going to the doctor made me feel better, although it was really only a placebo effect. Primarily, it was the care I received that helped me the most. The doctors and staff were caring and compassionate, which made a significant difference to my experience. I'd always been drawn to certain people on a spiritual level and instinctively knew that these people truly cared for me.

Despite seeing countless specialists called in because of the unusual nature of my case, none could pinpoint the cause. I lost track of the tests, medications, and procedures I endured. After a while, all the faces and names of the doctors became a blur. At times I felt like a lab animal. All I wanted to was break free from the confinement of hospitals and clinics. Never once did I have the same experience as far as treatment, diagnosis, etc., were concerned. It became an exhausting, endless ordeal.

My mother was my rock during these endless visits. She performed meditative prayer when she was with me and was my watchdog, always asking questions, always seeking answers. Her faith, wisdom, and love sustained me mentally and physically. She was my counsellor, friend, and advisor. Do right by all and it would return to you, she often said.

Some of the specialists suggested trying a laser procedure on my eyes as a last resort. It was the early eighties and the technology was still quite new and considered experimental. After consultation with the doctors, my family decided that the procedure was too risky. Surgery was another option, but my mother didn't want to pursue such an extreme option.

By that point she was extremely concerned about my condition. None of the treatments work. Nor did any of the prescriptions, including the painkillers, which made me sick. She'd always assured me that God would help me and that I wouldn't have to deal with this all my life, but now she felt it was time to take action. Believing that faith would find a way, she enlisted the help of friends and the older people in our community to pray for my healing.

Remarkably, after much prayer, God manifested miracle. My eyesight improved and the pain started subsided in one eye. I'd mostly recovered by the time I was fourteen, but my full sight didn't completely return until I was fifteen.

CHAPTER 4

My Road to Damascus

When I was twenty-five, I experienced a life-changing event. A road to Damascus moment, if you will. This catalyst further propelled me toward my calling as a minister of God. I was involved in a head-on car accident that I should never have survived. The driver of the other was was killed instantly. To this day, rescue workers, hospital staff, and anyone who was involved in or knew of the accident called my survival a miracle.

Admittedly, it was my transgression against God that caused it. He even warned me about his punishment a week before when I was involved a minor accident. But even though I felt the spirit of death around me, I didn't heed his message.

I allowed my weakness for women to push me to the brink of death. As such, I had many girlfriends. Despite my relationship with Sheila, I succumbed to temptation and was seeing another woman. One the day of the accident I was driving to the country to meet her.

The memory remains blurry like images in the fog. It was as though I was sitting in a theater watching a movie of the event rather than an actual participant. I collided head on with another car. There was a tremendous impact and then the hellish impact of metal screeching against metal moments before I blacked out. When I briefly regained consciousness, I remember excruciating pain and the sound of a helicopter hovering overhead. I believe I did die for a short time, but I didn't see the visions I normally experienced. In fact, I saw nothing at all.

I was told the car was a mangled wreck. Rescue workers had to cut me out with the jaws of life. The engine of the other car had crushed me, severing my legs and caving in my chest. Practically every bone in my body was broken. I was rushed to a trauma center and placed on life support where I remained in a coma for a week. Medical staff were so certain I was going to die they recommended removing me from life support.

Of course my mother wouldn't hear of it. She prayed for God's help and to the astonishment of the medical staff, I woke up. Everyone believed it was a miracle that opened my eyes, especially considering that one of my cousin's had recently died from the same type of accident. But although I'd survived, the pain I experienced when I did wake up was agonizing. I had plates in my arms and rods in my hips. One of my hands was larger than the other and to this day my arm looks deformed.

The doctors said I'd never walk again, but God healed me. Through prayer and determination, I took my first step two years later and started working, even though I could do very little. While I was in rehab for a while, the therapists wanted to use pool therapy and because I couldn't swim, I stopped going. I recovered with my mother for over a year then stayed with Sheila for a while. From crawling, I moved onto a walker and then gradually regained my ability to walk. The journey to recovery took four years after the accident.

I was fortunate enough to sustain no longstanding issues from those catastrophic injuries apart from some aches and pains. What did remain was the legacy of pain and suffering that had marked my life. This provided me the tools that I would use in my mission as a minister of God to reach and counsel those also enduing trauma. Much like radar, I sensed the feelings of others.

By using my trauma as an example, I would go on to give people the hope to keep going and the strength not to not give up. It was my destiny to show those drowning in hopelessness and despair or those considering suicide that there was someone out there who cared. I had become a spiritual doctor forever on call.

Finally, I had accepted my calling as a warrior of God.

CHAPTER 5

Depression

Unfortunately, I would suffer from yet another torment that would push me to the brink of despair and suicide. From 1991 to 2004, depression darkened the light from the sky and my mind. Though the sun rose in the sky every morning, my endless suffering and trauma opened the gateway to a darkness that would become a suffocating veil of depression. To always be sick, weak, uncomfortable, frightened, overwhelmed, unable to sleep...to deal with low self-esteem and watch life pass me by...the laundry list of my ordeal seemed endless.

Yes, I was a fighter, yes my faith was strong. Prayer was my salvation, the glory of God my anchor. But I was also flesh and blood, a child robbed of his health and what should have been a carefree youth. The struggle continued through my teen years and affected my daily life.

Of course I realized that my depression was fueled by supernatural forces that sought to weaken and destroy me. There were days I could barely cope, days I was imprisoned by my poor health and inability to function normally like others. It seemed the older I got the more frequent the visitations became. Like vermin, the demons lingered in the shadows, watching, waiting, attacking me at every opportunity.

While my asthma and vision issues were torment enough, depression was more insidious as it affected my physical and mental health. The anxiety and fear I experienced at times was so overwhelming that I often shook and broke out in a cold sweat. I suffered from heart palpitations and frequently hyperventilated, which only aggravated the breathing issues caused by my asthma. My appearance reflected what I was going through.

As for the despair and feelings of hopelessness, only someone who has experienced depression can truly understand what it was like to be trapped in such a dark place. No one could endure so much without becoming depressed or reaching a breaking point, and eventually, my thoughts became suicidal. While I knew that taking my own life was a crime against God, the demons haunting me used those thoughts to whittle away at my resolve.

But in my usual determined way, I found a way to hide my suffering and kept going. I tried to be as active as possible through working with my brother in his home improvement business. Athletics also helped. I participated in kickboxing, running, weightlifting, basketball, and football, but these activities only took me so far because I suffered from a a spiritual affliction as well. Being outside, being elsewhere, occupying myself with tasks that required focusing away from my suffering helped divert the voices whispering in my mind.

I never sought medical treatment for my depression. My life was already consumed with illness and doctors' visits. Nor did I talk about it with anyone besides my mother and sometimes my aunt in Ohio. My mother was my constant guiding light and I only felt comfortable confiding in her about my issues. Her love and faith supported and guided me through these difficult times.

I also found talking with the older people in the community helped me and I benefited from their wisdom. At the very core of my suffering, at the lowest place I descended through the dark days, I remembered that God had called me to an important task.

Even though many people in the community weren't well-educated, those living in the country lived a simpler life that was far more connected to nature and the presence of God. We were always aware of nature and the essence of life and appreciated our daily blessings. Stripped of the hustle of city life and superficial concerns, the people I had grown up around proved to be the greatest support when I needed them.

In reality few would have believed me even if I had been more open about my experiences since birth. It was God's way of preparing me for my calling as a minister. This preparation was put to the test when I foresaw my mother's death in 2003. I not only foresaw it, but I felt it. My mother had almost died two years earlier, but I had prayed by her bedside and asked God to save her. In exchange, I promised to serve Him.

CHAPTER 6

Spiritual Warfare

As I came to accept my calling, I became more attuned to the darkness following me. It was similar to the ability to see auras. Only I could sense the unnatural shifts in energy around me. I also experienced prescience and knew when things would happen and to whom long before anyone else.

The more I awakened to God's calling the more other forces became aware of my gifts. I came to recognize them as demonic forces intent on preying on me, physically weakening me, and wearing me down spiritually.

Evil spirits, or negative energies, thrive in conditions that breed poverty, addiction, hopelessness, despair, and depression. They are the causes of most disease, which stems from an infection of the spirit. They feed on those suffering physically and mentally. Particularly, those floundering in the depths of depression. These are their gathering places to harvest as many souls into darkness as they can. Misery loves company. And, children like me were prime targets.

The more these forces haunted me, I saw and heard them, often times having to fight them off. This was only the beginning of many tests and sacrifices I would have to make to serve God and hone my abilities sharply enough to deliver others from this darkness, as a champion of light.

Many psychic attacks and forms of spiritual warfare

manifest themselves in physical afflictions. I found this to be true more than once over the course of my life. Especially, when I was afflicted by an attack that took the form of something far worse than the most severe form of eczema. Like Job, I was afflicted by boils on my skin that dried out, causing my skin to peel, and leaving me with unsightly scabs.

The condition, of course, deeply affected my confidence and self-esteem lowering my vibrations. Which was the purpose of this attack all along. Not surprisingly, like with the loss of my sight, no doctors could find the cause or necessarily the cure for any of it.

This being the one of many straws that could have possibly broken the camels back, the skin affliction finally did. My absences from school due to my health had caught up with me and I was forced to drop out in my junior year.

— ⟨◎⟩ —

CHAPTER 7

The Gift of Discernment, Empathy, and Healing

The gifts of discernment, empathy, and healing are often given as a trinity. They play a very integral role in each other's potency. This is why if someone is gifted with one, more times than not, they will discover they possess the others as well.

Discernment, or intuition as it is called in some circles, is the gift of Knowing. Not to be mistaken for the gift of Wisdom, just because you know something does not make you wise. It only makes you smart. You may have a tool, but if you do not understand how to use it; it is useless in your hands.

Having the gift of discernment, much of the time will manifest itself in small quiet ways. Such as, knowing how others are feeling. Sometimes it will show itself in bigger ways; for example being able to see the future. Or receiving messages and visitation from other supernatural beings. This can be in the forms of visions, voices (either in your mind or audible), or physical visitations. For those who do not understand right at first, this can be very disconcerting and you may think you are losing your mind. I'm here to reassure you, you are not.

In the beginning of my life, before I truly realized God had honored me with this gift. A gift I could strengthen and hone. It frightened me quite a lot. Especially, as a child; before I grew and reached my spiritual awakening. Seeing God had chosen me as a discerner to deliver His message of love to the world in miracles through the power of belief. Once I saw it was my duty to fulfill this mission. The possession of this gift frightened me less and less.

For those of you with the gift of Empathy, you understand it is the ability to take on the feelings and energies of others around you. This can also be quite disconcerting in the beginning. Because, more often than not, it will manifest itself in the manner of sudden mood swings, changes in behavior, and sometimes even sudden illness or outward physical afflictions. A lot of the time these illnesses and physical afflictions are attacks or maladies on the souls and minds of those you spend the most time around. This is why they affect you more than others, because you are spiritually hypersensitive. Much as I was, when I was a child. Most with the gift of Empathy manifest their gift early and are often just mistaken for being sickly or frail children. Those who move into adulthood without realizing their gift, often will mistake their symptoms for anxiety, chronic depression, and bipolar. Leaving the door open for demonic forces, who love nothing more than to encourage these false perceptions of self; in order to discourage you and make you feel less than worthy because you believe you have a mental illness. Until, the time of my healing and rebirth in Christ I was very much a victim of these atrocities.

The best way to realize you have been given the gift of

Empathy is to take the time to sit down and ask yourself these simple questions.

Do you emotionally absorb the energy of a room, when you walk into a group?

Do you often know there is more to a story than someone is telling you?

Are you a human lie detector?

Do you feel emotionally drained by crowds and need time alone to recharge?

Do conflicting smells, excessive noise, and mindless chatter fray your nerves?

Do people, even complete strangers, feel compelled to tell you the truth or their "life story", things they have never revealed to anyone?

Do you have trouble setting boundaries without feeling excessively guilty because you are afraid of feeling rejection or disapproval?

Do you take on too much, for the same reason as the previous question, then sabotage yourself for fear of being overwhelmed?

If you can answer "yes" to any of these questions. Then, you have been given the gift of Empathy. Although, in the beginning, it can feel like a bit of a burden rather than a blessing. Once you take the steps to truly see that what you have been blessed with is a gift, you will be able to more effectively add value to your life and the lives of others, as I have.

Empathy, perhaps is the most important ingredient in this trinity of abilities; because it is the ability to take on others feelings, energies, and physical afflictions as your own in order to better serve them. This leads directly into the third and final gift. The gift of Healing.

Healing through the power of God's love, is something I have been more than fortunate to experience for myself. As I stated in the first chapter, it was a great time of rebirth for me. Literally, giving me a new lease on life and showing me my true path and purpose as a light bringer.

Throughout the Bible, we see many accounts of healing through faith and God's love. The most frequent of these accounts, of course, are the one's of Jesus doing as He was prophesied to do. "The blind receive sight, the lame walk, the lepers are cleansed, the deaf hear, the dead are raised, and good news is preached to the poor." Matthew 11:5

As the Son of God, the visitation of God in human flesh, He possessed the power to heal afflictions and drive out evil spirits; even, from long distances. Or just through the faith of the individual receiving the healing, because He is God.

"Surely He took on our infirmities and carried our sorrows; yet we considered Him stricken by God, struck down and afflicted." Isaiah 53:4

Because we are made in God's image, the affect is very much the same on the body of a faith healer. Through empathy you take on the infirmity of the one in need. Whether it be mental, physical, or spiritual. Then, through faith and God's omnipotent love the affliction is transformed within you. And, by praying, the laying on of hands, and anointing of oil the malady is replaced by God's renewing light and love. As it did for me, this experience can and will change a person's entire life.

When you are a healer, you possess the power to give

others a new start. Just as becoming a parent, a creator of life, is nothing to take lightly. This gift should be approached with the same amount of reverence and pause. By giving you this ability, God has entrusted you with one of His most precious of gifts. Once I saw and felt with every fiber of my being, the true power of God through this gift. I realized just how important my mission really is.

Chapter 8

- ⟨❦⟩ -

Sacrificing My Gifts to Bring Value to Others

Since my anointing, I felt surrounded by a divine presence and others noticed. Everything and everyone I touched felt God's presence. When I touched people I gave them healing life through the Holy Spirit.

I've defied doctors by saving hundreds from disease, suicide, injuries, depression, demonic possession, and other dark arts. I've witnessed people healed and able to walk again thanks to the power of God. Everyday I saw new miracles. I prayed and provided grief counseling for thousands of people around the world in person and through my prayer line.

It didn't matter what race, religion or economic status. It didn't matter whether people were wealthy or homeless. I particularly help a special place in my heart for women because of their strength and the burdens they endured. I made spiritual house calls to homes, hospitals, churches, hospices, and many other places to help the suffering and tormented. I went on the road to attend revivals and even helped those in war zones.

God made me His agent to deliver a message of hope and to bring His light to the billions of people around the world. And, I wanted to start first by lighting the flame of hope in your heart by the story of my inspired journey through hardship and victory in Jesus Christ. Such is the power of the Holy Spirit!

CHAPTER 9

I Have Seen Miracles

Testimonials

Testimonial of Edward Piper, Montevallo, Alabama, March 5, 2005, as witnessed by Timothy Young

My brother and I received a phone call requesting an estimate for home improvement. When we arrived at the residence, no one answered the door so we went to the neighbor's house to inquire. The woman's grandson, Edward Piper, crawled through the neighbor's window and opened the door. Inside the house we were shocked to find a woman in her fifties whose body was literally twisted into a pretzel.

Her face was a mask of horror with skin hanging from her face. Amazingly, she had been battling bone cancer for eighteen years and had suffered endless pain and anguish. She told us she had been to the best specialists and had done all she could just like the woman in the Bible with the issue of blood.

I asked her if I could pray for her and she said yes. We asked her to repent. As I prayed for her I felt all her pain. A few moments later her arms and legs began to straighten, her skin molded back onto her face and the pain drained from her body. God had created a new human being before us. She was able to laugh and held up her hand. She kicked her leg and turned her head to shout, "Thank you, God!" We were all astonished by her transformation.

Testimonial of Brenda Wanger, Oklahoma City, Oklahoma, February 8, 2008

Yes, to my recollection, we were at a revival and Pastor Tim asked people to come up for prayer. A woman we'll call June came up and as Pastor Tim began to pray for her, she began to laugh and grin demonically. When she began to levitate, Pastor Tim prayed against the demonic manifestation. Her face transformed into a demonic mask. While the Pastor battled these demons, I saw fourteen angels surround him. Their hands were upon him as he prayed. When June dropped back onto the floor her face was normal. She was so happy that she had been delivered. Then the angels disappeared. The whole church was astonished.

Testimonial of Linda Eaton, Gardendale, Alabama, January 8, 2012

I received a call from my daughter who asked if I knew anyone that could help an elderly woman and her granddaughter who were under demonic attack. The woman used to be a Wiccan and used a Ouija board. I told her I'd call Pastor Tim and Pastor Geddis. When I called Pastor Tim and told him about the situation, he told us he could come in five days.

The situation became quite dangerous after that. Not only was Pastor Tim attacked, but both their vehicles had mysteriously broken down. That Saturday I had to pick them up. When we arrived at the elderly woman's house around 10.30 am, you could feel an oppressively heavy, demonic presence. After we rang the doorbell, the woman's granddaughter opened the door. She looked like the girl in the exorcist and was dressed in black. Even her eyes were black. Never once did she take her eyes off Pastor Tim as he came into the house.

There were several other people already at the house. The elderly woman was almost paralyzed. We all began to pray and Pastor Tim began to bind up the dark, demonic spirits that had been summoned through the Ouija board. Then Pastor Tim grabbed the granddaughter and began to pray and call out the name of Jesus. At that moment we heard a series of what sounded like explosions throughout the house.

As soon as the girl was released from the demonic spirits, the room began to light up. Pastor Tim then prayed for the grandmother, who was able to walk. Afterward he went to the basement where the demonic presence was the strongest and cleared it from the house.

TRIBUTES & MEMORIALS

First and foremost I would like to pay tribute to my Lord and Savior Jesus Christ. The one who called me to this truly incredible ministry and has brought so much value to my life, by allowing me to bring value to the life of so many others through my gift. Praise be to God!

Also, my mother Ella Mae Rand, a true embodiment of the Lord Jesus here on earth. Who tirelessly prayed for me, gave me life, and gave me Jesus. Thank you, Mama.

I would also like to pay tribute to all of the others in my life who have been there for me. Supporting me, believing in me, loving me, and lifting me up as true members of the body of Christ.

My Sister, Barbara
Jackie
Pastor Miller
Paul Kim Molina
My Wife, Sheila
Daughter, Jasmine
Pastor Morgon
Sister, Janet
V Gilchrist
Brother, Romero
And a special tribute to all the Saints in Christ
You know who you are.

CONTACT ME

For all of you who are weary and heavy laden,
seeking hope and the light it brings.
Feel free to contact me here at my
worldwide prayer and crisis line.
www.prayerandhope.org
So no matter where you are in the world, or place you
are in your life, let me be the helping and reassuring
hand to guide you back to the light of hope.

Finding Your Ray of Hope
Through Jesus Christ

An Invitation to Prayer and Personal
Relationship with Jesus Christ

If you would like to give your heart to
Jesus Christ, repeat after me.
I acknowledge that you, Jesus, are the Son of God. I
believe that you died on the cross, that your blood was
shed for my sins and that you arose from the grave
and conquered death. I understand that I was born
a sinner and that I have sinned by disobeying your
commandments. I ask you to forgive me for these sins.
Please change my heart to be like yours-loving and full of
forgiveness. Help me to obey your teachings as recorded
in the Bible. Bring people who can help me on this new
path. Be my Savior. Be my Lord. Thank you for saving
me from death and giving me new life and hope, Amen.

Printed in the United States
By Bookmasters